Face the facts

Tongue?

Game face

and nail

No skin off my nose

Eyes in the back of his

By the skin of

Tripped on his tongue

Deep

Bird's-eye view

ne face

is head

Beauty is only skin de

I'm all ears

Fly in the face

Face the fact

eyeball

bs his nose

My lips are sealed

ied

Apple of my eye

I'm all ears

In the blink of an eye

eye on you

Beauty is only skin deep

ose on your face

Lend me your ears

Keep a stiff upper lip

t giving you lip

Pull the wool over your eye

Fly in the face of

Poker face

n your fa

Beauty is only skin deep

lk your ear off

Nose in th

cat got

Game face

Eye for an eye

in the

face

Right under your nose

his tongue

Apple

his tongue

Face to face

Poke

all ears

Turn the other cheek

Stone-faced

face

ve face

Tongue-tie

ose clean

Wet behind the ears

t got your tongue

Thumbs his nose

t giving you lip

service

In Your Face

The **FACTS** about Your Features

Donna M. Jackson

VIKING

VIKING

Published by Penguin Group

Penguin Young Readers Group, 345 Hudson Street, New York, New York 10014, U.S.A.

Penguin Books Ltd, 80 Strand, London WC2R 0RL, England

Penguin Books Australia Ltd, 250 Camberwell Road, Camberwell, Victoria 3124, Australia

Penguin Books Canada Ltd, 10 Alcorn Avenue, Toronto, Ontario, Canada M4V 3B2

Penguin Books (N.Z.) Ltd, 182-190 Wairau Road, Auckland 10, New Zealand

First published in 2004 by Viking, a division of Penguin Young Readers Group

1 3 5 7 9 10 8 6 4 2

LIBRARY OF CONGRESS CATALOGING-IN-PUBLICATION DATA

Jackson, Donna M., date.

In your face : the facts about your features / by Donna M. Jackson.

p. cm.

Includes bibliographical references and index.

ISBN 0-670-03657-9 (hardcover)

1. Face—Juvenile literature. 2. Face perception—Juvenile literature. 3. Face (Philosophy)—Juvenile literature. [1. Face.] I. Title.

QM535.J33 2004   611'.92—dc22   2003026331

Manufactured in China

Set in Egyptienne

Book design by Nancy Brennan

PHOTO CREDITS

Front jacket photo, pages 3, 4, 5, 6, and 21, copyright © 2004 Getty Images; Title page, copyright © 2003 PhotoNewZealand.com; Pages 1, 29, and back jacket, copyright © 2004 CORBIS; Pages 2 and 23, copyright © 2004 AP Wide World Photos; Page 8, courtesy of the Gene Astorino family; Page 9, copyright © 2004 Brand X Pictures/Say Cheese Company; Page 10, courtesy of Shelley King Frihauf and the King family; Page 11, courtesy of Michael Gates and family; Page 13, courtesy of the Shoemaker family and the National Center for Missing and Exploited Children (www.missingkids.com); Page 15, caricature copyright © 2004 Dan Smith; Pages 17 and 18, courtesy of Hans and Cecilia Burman; Page 26, courtesy of Dan and Sharon Deveney and family; Page 30, courtesy of Bob and Lori Chasse and family; Page 31, used with the permission of the Alexander Turnbull Library, National Library of New Zealand Te Puna Matauranga o Aotearoa; Page 35, courtesy of David Trainer, Factor II, Inc.; Page 36, courtesy of Barbara Spohn-Lillo, Prosthetic Illusions, Rocky Mountain Anaplastology, Inc.

To my godchildren Crystal, Tiffany, and Lauren,
three beautiful girls whose faces I love dearly.

• • • • • •

Acknowledgments

MANY THANKS TO ALL those who took the time to share their work for the book: Barbara Spohn-Lillo at Prosthetic Illusions; Vicki and Sean McCarrell of the Moebius Syndrome Foundation; Dan, Sharon, and Lauren Deveney; Hans and Cecilia Burman; Jim Cooke; Dr. Bradley Duchaine at the Vision Sciences Lab, Harvard University; Steve Loftin, S. Orname Thompson, and D'Ann Taflin at the National Center for Missing and Exploited Children; David Trainer at Factor II, Inc.; Gayle and Michael Munds; Dr. Leslie Lebrowitz at Brandeis University; Dr. Paul Ekman at the University of California Medical School, San Francisco; Dr. David Matsumoto of the Culture and Emotion Research Lab at San Francisco State University; Sloane Miller at Times Books; Gerry Leary; Meir Kahtan at Identix, Inc.; Beverly Griffin at Griffin Investigations; Dan and Shelley Frihauf and family; Michael Gates; Camille Ruggiero at AP Wide World Photos; Chris Jackson and Kari Evancich; Robert and Lori Chasse and family; Dr. Steven Denenberg at www.facialsurgery.com/PPghome_page.html; Greg, Ying, and Vinson Compestine; Charles S. Kline, photographic archivist, University of Pennsylvania Museum of Archaeology and Anthropology; Lisa McQueen at PhotoNewZealand.com; Gary B. Meisner, Phi scholar at www.goldennumber.net; Carmel Zuker and Marty Caivano of the *Boulder Daily Camera*; Tony Rubalcava at Copley News Service; Mark Katzman at the American Museum of Natural History; caricaturist Dan Smith; Betty Moss of the Alexander Turnbull Library, National Library of New Zealand; and Vic and Nettie Shoemaker.

Special thanks to Elizabeth Law for clearing the path to Viking; to Catherine Frank, for patiently waiting for me and providing superb editorial guidance; and to Charlie and Christopher Jackson, for being my Northern Star—yours are the two faces I love seeing most in the world.

For news of the heart, ask the face.

—*Guinean proverb*

CONTENTS

ABOUT FACE

FISH FACES. That's pretty much how we began, say scientists. Our human faces originated in the sea about 500 million years ago with the rise of creatures such as the Pikaia (pih-KAY-ah)—a wormlike animal about one-and-a-half inches long that swam above the ocean floor. Unlike their passive predecessors, these sea animals possessed an opening on one end that allowed them to take in water and sift food from it. This primitive mouth led to the development of creatures with primitive eyes that directed them to food, primitive noses that distinguished among odors, and primitive jaws that closed their mouths and kept food from floating away.

Scientists say our faces originated in the sea about 500 million years ago. Pictured is a Garibaldi fish.

As time passed, the animals most efficient at finding food outlived their competitors. And nature handed down a facial pattern to ensure success: two eyes, a nose, and a mouth, shaped in a T formation. While variations within species exist, these features are strategically placed for survival in most animals so that as the mouth consumes food, the eyes and nose above it can watch for and sniff out danger.

Fast-forward through time—past the first reptiles who crawled out of the water and breathed air through tiny nostrils, past the early mammals whose mouth muscles formed the first facial expressions, and past the apes who commanded powerful jaws for chewing prey—to 5 million years ago when our early ancestors began walking upright on two feet. No longer did the face need to be a weapon, with a jutting jaw and giant teeth to slice meat. As hundreds of thousands of years unfolded, our faces flattened, our foreheads expanded to house our growing brains, our noses projected and our chins emerged. With the advent of *Homo sapiens* about 100,000 years ago, the modern-day human face was born.

Chimpanzees have smaller skulls than humans and faces with muzzles and flat noses. Human faces display prominent chins and projecting noses.

· · · · · ·

Tour de Face

WHAT DISTINGUISHES our faces from those of other mammals? Specifically, our lack of heavy facial hair. "Our faces are bare so others can read them," says Daniel McNeill, author of *The Face*. "In most mammals, the upper lip clings tightly to the gums.... But in monkeys [and humans] the upper lip is free and moves about deftly."

Having a free upper lip allows our faces to take different shapes and enables us to exchange sophisticated facial expressions that are essential to our socialization—

something we couldn't do behind a mask of hair. "Our ability to gauge trust and work with others depends partly on the face. . . . It has let us farm, mine, and wire the earth," says McNeill. "The hairless face was a first step to civilization."

The Mouth

SMILES, SIGHS, pouts, and yawns. All spring from the mouth, which not only conveys a wide array of feelings, but also prevents us from starving. The mouth eats, drinks, talks, and tastes. It dominates the face in most animals and is the first facial organ to form in human embryos. Interestingly, the human mouth is narrower than that of most other animals, possibly to keep contaminants out, says McNeill.

Our mouths enable us to express many feelings. our lips come in handy for kissing, and our tongue helps us to swallow food.

The lips also work to protect our mouth from unwanted materials. They're extremely sensitive and can detect a single hair trying to sneak in. While women's lips are generally fuller than men's, both amplify facial expressions and reveal clues as to what people are trying to tell us.

Lining the mouth are our teeth, which gleam when we smile and capture people's attention. They're the strongest parts of our face. The tongue—made up of many muscles—helps us to swallow, which we do about once a minute when we're not eating and about nine times a minute when we are, says McNeill. As for our chins, they remain a mystery with no clearly defined purpose except to sharpen our profiles.

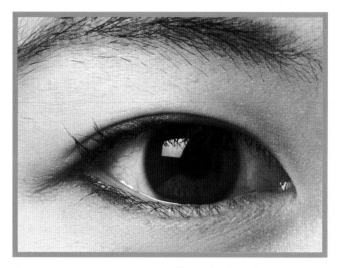

Our eyes are often the first facial feature to capture people's attention. They blink an average of 4,200,000 times a year to keep moist.

The Eyes

BROWN EYES. Blue eyes. Green eyes. "The eyes are the most powerful and intimate part of the face," says McNeill. The visible portion of the eye has three interacting parts: the white, the iris, and the pupil. The iris, which gives our eyes their color, is a beautiful pair of muscles that works like a shutter and controls how much light can enter the eye through the pupil. In the sun, the iris shrinks the pupil; in the dark, it expands it. The white part of the eye sits in the background and contrasts with the iris and the pupil to highlight their movements and send out a constant stream of messages.

One message it conveys is where our attention is focused. Are you paying attention to the teacher or are you gazing just beyond the classroom door, waiting for the bell to ring? Your eyes can give you away. They also can steal about twenty-three minutes of your day by blinking. It's estimated that the human eye blinks an average of 4,200,000 times a year, all in an effort to keep moist like our fish-faced ancestors' eyes.

Framing our eyes are eyebrows—one of our most distinctive and expressive features. Some scientists believe that eyebrows may have helped our ancestors survive by keeping rain and sweat out of their eyes when predators chased them. Today, we communicate everything from surprise to interest to anger by raising and lowering our eyebrows. Some people also pluck and shape their eyebrows to make their eyes appear larger.

The Nose

SITTING IN the center of our face is the nose, which grows throughout our lifetime and consists primarily of a tough elastic tissue called cartilage. Noses can vary from culture to culture and come in all shapes and sizes—flat, thin, wide, narrow, big tip, little tip, etc. One reason they often differ among cultures is environmental. Large, narrow noses work well in desert climates by giving air more time to moisten before it reaches the lungs, and short, broad noses work best in humid environments, where they move already moist air to the lungs more quickly.

"The nose's importance is reflected in our language," says plastic surgeon Dr. Steven Denenberg. "We may look down our nose at someone, or turn it up at something. Sometimes we can't see beyond it, or we even cut it off to spite our face. We keep it to the grindstone, poke it into other people's business, pay through it, and lead someone around by it. Someone may follow his nose, win by a nose, guess your age on the nose, rub noses with someone, or just be nosy. It's as plain as the nose on your face."

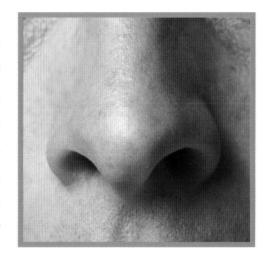

Our noses come in all shapes and sizes and are mostly made of cartilage.

The Skin

LIKE THE nose, our skin color is a response to our environment. Melanin—nature's sunscreen—colors our skin to protect it from burning in the sun: having a lot of melanin makes skin dark and having a little makes it lighter. Until about 100,000 years ago, our ancestors were all black-skinned in response to their environment—the sunny deserts of Africa. As people migrated out of Africa into colder, less sunny climates, their skin turned lighter to drink in more of the sun's rays and more easily produce vitamin D, which is necessary to absorb calcium and build strong bones.

The skin is our body's waterproof temperature regulator and protector against viruses and infections. It's the largest organ of the body, containing millions of nerves, glands, blood vessels and hair follicles. Every minute, thousands of skin cells flake away from our skin. (That's how dogs sniff us out!)

The thinnest skin on our bodies? It covers our eyelids.

Foreheads, Ears, and Hair

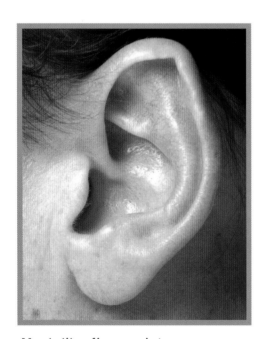

Much like fingerprints, our ears display unique patterns that can help others identify us.

OUR FOREHEADS top off our faces and are an area long associated with intellect. One reason may be because behind our forehead lies the part of the brain that controls emotions and decision-making: the frontal cortex. Men's foreheads typically slant back slightly, while women's rise upward. In India, people who belong to the Hindu religion wear a bright red vermilion mark on their forehead called a *Tilaka*. The *Tilaka*, which means "mark," comes in various shapes and sizes to correspond with the different Hindu sects. Some believe that the red color of the *Tilaka* symbolizes blood.

The ears sandwich our face, with flaps made of cartilage and lobes filled with fatty tissue. Like fingerprints, they carry a unique pattern—of contours and cartilage—that can be used for identification.

Framing our faces are about 100,000 strands of straight, curly, or wavy hair that we style in many different ways. The color, texture, and thickness of our hair is determined by our genes, as is whether or not we go bald. Genetics also decide how quickly and how long our hair grows. Generally, a teenager's hair grows faster than an adult's hair. In addition, ethnicity plays a role in determining the type of hair that grows on our heads: Asian hair is typically black and straight, while African hair is generally brown and kinky.

Beards and mustaches "may be the most baffling facial features of all," says *The Face* author, McNeill. Some scientists believe they're a leftover, primitive way of helping men show their virility and intimidating the competition. Alternatively, they may be here for deception—keeping people from reading the very facial signals that our smooth faces were designed to transmit.

Put together, our facial features form the basis of our fascinating faces—giving us a one-of-a-kind identity that we use to communicate with the world.

FACIAL IDENTITY

While identical twins share the same genes, their faces still differ to some degree.

SIX BILLION faces in the world, and like snowflakes, no two are exactly the same. Our faces help define who we are and make it easy for us to identify friends and family we want to keep close, as well as strangers we wish to avoid. Some of us look similar—we have our mother's eyes or our father's nose. Ultimately, however, our faces are the result of a one-of-a-kind melding of a great number of genes passed down to us through many generations. Even the faces of identical twins, who share the same genetic plans, differ to some degree. Environmental differences, both before and after birth, influence the features of the face.

First Impressions

UNLIKE DOGS, cats, and many other species, most humans recognize their own reflections. It takes about 18 months before we develop this ability, but once it is in place, we generally take it for granted. At around 19 months, we also begin to distinguish between male and female faces—with the help of a few clues from Mother Nature.

From birth, a boy's head is generally larger than a girl's. Men tend to have larger jaws than females, a relatively low, slanted forehead, and a thick, bony ridge above their eyes that makes the eyes appear deep-set. Men's eyebrows also grow heavier and their noses sit longer and wider in proportion to their face. With the onset of puberty, they grow facial hair and their skin coarsens in response to increased testosterone levels.

Nature makes babies especially attractive to trigger a nurturing response in caregivers.

Women, on the other hand, possess smooth-skinned faces on heads that typically are about two-thirds the size of a male's. A woman's forehead generally rises upward and her eyebrows sit higher, making her eyes seem larger and more prominent than a man's. Her lips and cheeks also are fuller, and her overall skin tone is usually lighter than that of the males of her race. This lighter skin may be nature's way of indicating fertility, because a woman's skin darkens during pregnancy.

Faces not only reveal our gender, they give away our age. Babies, for example, typically have faces with plump cheeks, large foreheads, small chins, wide eyes, and turned-up noses. Nature makes infants especially appealing so adults will nurture them until they can survive on their own. As babies grow and become less dependent on adults for survival, their faces mature and become more childlike, often with missing teeth and freckles. Teenagers and young adults have faces some consider to be at the peak of their beauty, while adult faces generally look "mature," with proportionally

The Aging Process

1 Henry A. King as a toddler.

2 12 years old in 1918.

3 A 22-year-old medical student in 1928.

4 36 years old in the Army Medical Corps in 1942.

5 62 years old in 1968.

smaller foreheads and eyes, and more prominent cheeks and chins than baby faces.

Along with age and gender, faces indicate whether people are healthy and fit—physically and mentally. They also influence who we choose as a mate. One study by David Perrett of St. Andrews University in Scotland showed that the faces we find most attractive resemble our own. We may have a natural instinct to pair with people who look like our parents, he says, since theirs are the first faces we see regularly as an infant. A different study by researcher Anthony Little showed that "people generally prefer faces with the same eye and hair color as their parent of the opposite sex." For example, a woman is more likely to be attracted to a man with blue eyes and brown hair if her father possesses similar features.

Overgeneralizing Traits

"DON'T JUDGE a book by its cover," goes the old saying. But that's exactly what most of us do when we first meet a person. While facial clues help us instinctively distinguish between men and women, the old and the young, and the sick and the healthy, the information we pick up can sometimes be misleading—especially when we decide a person's character based on their face.

Our protective response to a baby's face, for example, is so strong that it often extends to adults who have baby-face features, says psychologist Leslie Zebrowitz, author of *Reading Faces*. "Adults who have relatively small chins or big eyes, round faces or small nose bridges often are perceived as having the kinds of traits that babies possess." We see them as warm, approachable, innocent, and less quarrelsome than people with "mature" faces, she says.

Being baby-faced may initially win people over, but it also can work against a person because of the contrast effect, explains Dr. Zebrowitz. "If you have two people who have equally cold personalities, the one who is baby-faced would be perceived as colder than the mature-faced person, because it's a contrast from our expectations." Since we expect baby-faced people to be kind, they disappoint us even more than mature-faced people when they're not.

The same overgeneralization effect typically holds true for people whose features look like an emotion. "The person whose mouth naturally turns up at the corners may be perceived as happy, and the person with low-placed eyebrows may be perceived as angry," says Dr. Zebrowitz.

Adults with "baby faces" often are viewed by others as warmer and more approachable.

There's even an animal overgeneralization effect, where people with animal-like features are associated with certain character traits. In one study, "foxes and fox-faced men were judged as shrewd, whereas lions and lion-faced men were seen as dominant and proud."

The bottom line is that "we make snap judgments about people based on what they look like, even though we're taught not to do it, and we know that we shouldn't," says Dr. Zebrowitz. "There's a very strong pull to do it—nevertheless, it's important for people to be aware that it's happening and to check themselves, because their conclusions could be wrong. They may be trusting someone who is baby-faced, for example, when they shouldn't."

· · · · · ·

Missing Faces

OUR FIRST impressions of people originate from the face, but what happens when the face belongs to a missing child—one whose facial features are still developing? How do we project what the child's face will look like one, two, or ten years down the line? One way is to age-progress the face—a technique that organizations such as the National Center for Missing & Exploited Children (NCMEC) employ to help them find children who have been missing for a number of years.

"After some time has passed, it's very hard for people to picture what a toddler would look like as a ten- or thirteen-year-old and be able to recognize them," says forensic imaging specialist Steve Loftin. "By developing an image that's close to capturing some of the [present] characteristics of the child, we hope to provide enough information so that someone who sees the child will at least question who it is."

Five-year-old Victor Shoemaker, Jr., disappeared in May 1994 while playing with his cousins in a wooded area near Short Mountain in Kirby, West Virginia. Victor,

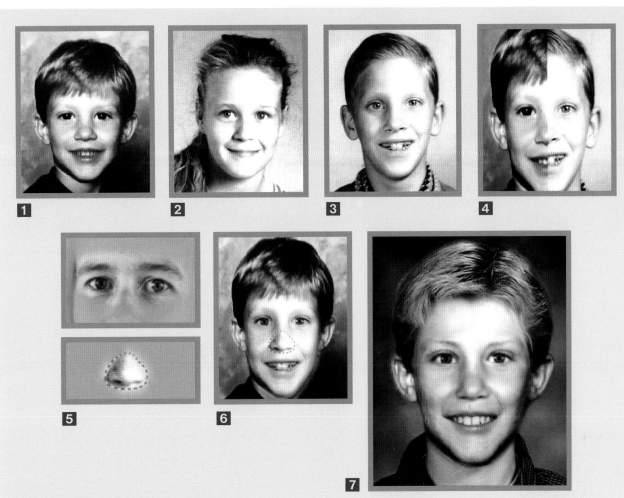

1 Victor Shoemaker, age five.

2 and **3** Photos of Victor's parents as children add to the accuracy of the age-progression process.

4 The forensic imaging specialist approximates facial growth for Victor's current age and "stretches" the face appropriately. Then he merges features from Victor's parents. This split image shows how he merged Victor's face with his dad's face as a child.

5 and **6** Victor's eyes and nose were similar to his mom's features, so they were merged with his image.

7 Victor's face progressed to age thirteen.

who was last seen wearing a red T-shirt and red shorts, told his cousins he was hungry and heading back to his grandfather's house, whom he was visiting with his parents. No one has seen him since.

To help locate Victor after all these years, a forensic imaging specialist at NCMEC age-progressed his face from age five to thirteen using information from the boy's family and photo-imaging software. "The first thing we do is collect photos of the parents and siblings, preferably those taken at around the same age we're trying to capture," says Loftin. This helps him to compare and contrast features.

Next, he takes the last image available of the child and "grows" the face on the computer. "Most of the growth in a child's face occurs in the lower two-thirds, while the eyes and the top portion of the skull change little," says Loftin. After "stretching out" the face, he merges it with another family member's image—in Victor's case, his dad's. Individual features from his mother and brothers and sisters are added as appropriate. If Victor had "his mother's nose," for example, Loftin would blend it with the image.

"The process involves a mix of art, science, and knowledge of heredity, facial growth, and the maturing of facial features," says an NCMEC spokesperson. From 1990 through January 2004, the organization created more than 2,180 age progressions, which played a role in the location of 453 children. Unfortunately, as of this printing, Victor Shoemaker remains missing.

* * * * * *

Facial Recognition

THE ABILITY to recognize ourselves and the faces of others—friends, family, celebrities, and acquaintances—affects our lives in profound ways. But how does the brain distinguish among all the different faces we see in a lifetime? Are we just the boy with freckles and green eyes or the girl with wavy brown hair?

Not at all, according to researchers. Our brains process faces as a whole, noting overall patterns of light and dark as well as the spacing and relationship among our features. Light and shadow provide the three-dimensional view we need to distinguish among the subtle details (curves, angles, shapes) of the face. This is why it's difficult for us to recognize someone solely from a line drawing.

Distinctive features—noses, ears, chins that set people apart from the average—also help the brain recognize and remember faces, especially if they belong to famous people or those we've recently met. Caricaturists who exaggerate celebrities' distinct features in their drawings use this knowledge to trigger instant recognition of their subjects. Caricatures of Prince Charles, for example, exaggerate the size of his ears, while caricatures of comedian Jay Leno emphasize the length of his chin.

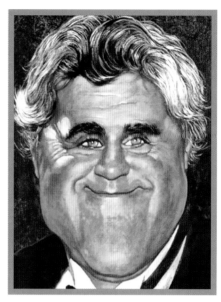

This caricature of Jay Leno emphasizes his long face and chin.

* * * * * *

Faceprints

NO DOUBT, our faces are unique—so unique that computers can tell them apart in a crowd. Today, with facial recognition technologies, banks verify Automated Teller Machine (ATM) users; casinos identify cheating gamblers; and cities such as Virginia Beach, Virginia, spot criminals and missing children in busy outdoor venues. In 2001, officials even used the technology at Super Bowl XXXV in Tampa Bay, Florida, to scan the crowd of 100,000 for potential terrorists—an event that some people protested as an invasion of privacy, calling it the "Snooper Bowl."

Facial recognition technology is one of several applications in a scientific field called biometrics. Biometrics are automated ways of recognizing people based on biological or physical characteristics such as fingerprints, eye retinas and irises, voice patterns, palm prints, and faces.

One facial recognition tool, called FaceIt, identifies people by measuring the relative distances between landmarks on the face, such as the space between the eyes, the width of the nose, and the depth of the eye sockets. These measurements are mapped into a one-of-a-kind digital code, called a faceprint, which, within seconds, can be compared to millions of others stored in a database. Our faces have about 80 nodal points (landmarks), but FaceIt needs only about 14 to 22 for recognition, says Frances Zelazny of Identix, the company that makes FaceIt. "We concentrate on the inner region of the face, which runs from temple to temple and just over the lip. . . . This is the most stable, because if you grow a beard, put on glasses, put on weight, or age, that region tends not to be affected."

Using live or recorded video surveillance tape, FaceIt can detect a face, alone or in a crowd, up to 35 degrees in all directions. Changes in lighting, skin tone, facial expression, and hair do not affect it. That's important to private investigators like Beverly Griffin, who says cheaters in casinos often try to avoid being spotted by wearing baseball caps and dark glasses or by ducking their heads and turning from side to side.

The technology's even gone mobile. A hand-held tool called IBIS (identification-based information system) can verify the faces and fingerprints of people stopped for traffic or other violations. IBIS captures the images and transmits them to a database where they're checked against files of known and suspected criminals. If a match occurs, police proceed accordingly. If there's no match, the images are deleted.

UNFAMILIAR FACES

One special group of people has difficulty recognizing any faces. They are prosopagnostics, and until recently, their plight was a lonely and frustrating one.

CECILIA BURMAN sees her friends and family perfectly well. The problem is, she doesn't recognize their faces. Cecilia is one of a rare group of people who have a neurological condition called prosopagnosia, or face blindness. Prosopagnosia is derived from the Greek word for face (*prosopon*) combined with the medical term for recognition impairment (*agnosia*).

Normally when we see a person, our brain searches its library of known faces to try to find a match and identify the individual, explains Cecilia. "When it finds a match, it uses the identity to look up other information about the person, such as his or her name, the last time you met, and so on." Face blindness occurs when the areas in the brain that are responsible for identifying and recognizing

Cecilia Burman has a rare disorder called prosopagnosia, or face blindness.

This is a simulated view of what Cecilia sees of her husband Hans' face.

people fail, says Dr. Bradley Duchaine of the Vision Sciences Laboratory at Harvard University. The condition varies from case to case, with some people even having an inability to recognize their own reflection in a mirror. "No one knows exactly how or why this occurs."

In some cases, damage to the identity-processing areas of the brain is caused by a stroke or a head injury resulting from an accident. Other times, as in Cecilia's case, it's present at, or soon after, birth. "I was in the third grade when I realized that something was wrong," says the thirty-six-year-old native of Sweden. "I'd been with the same group of students for three years, and I looked around the classroom and found that I could only name three of my classmates. I suspect that my mother noticed there was something wrong, too, when we looked at my class photo, and I didn't recognize anybody."

Test after test left doctors baffled. Cecilia was smart and had normal vision—she just couldn't identify people she knew by looking at their faces. "I had a few close friends that I learned to recognize by other means," she says. "But beyond that, I worked terribly hard to try to hide the problem so I could fit in."

Whenever Cecilia tried to explain her problem to others, they didn't quite grasp what she was saying. "Oh yes, I have trouble remembering faces, too," they would insist, not realizing the seriousness of her condition. Some acquaintances thought she wasn't trying hard enough to remember them, or that she didn't care. "It was embarrassing," Cecilia says. "And very lonely. Most people think that if you can see something like a face, then you must also automatically know what you are seeing. The problem is that you *do* see a face—you just can't see who it is." Much as people who are color blind can see colors but can't tell them apart, people with prosopagnosia can see faces but can't tell them apart.

Search for Answers

THROUGH THE years, Cecilia compensated for her condition as best she could—at school, at work, and in her social life—but never knew exactly what was wrong. "I work every day of my life trying to recognize people," she says. Some of the techniques she uses to identify people include noting:

- **Age and gender:** "I see these features as well as most people."
- **General body shape, hair, and face:** "For me recognizing a face is the same process that non-face-blind people would use to recognize a stone or an elbow."
- **Perceived attitude or relationship:** "I judge this from the way someone greets me."
- **Time and place of meeting:** "I look for work mates at work, etc."
- **Sound of voice:** "Hearing the voice of the person usually helps."
- **Subject:** "What the person chooses to talk about."

"I have problems recognizing people I have seen only a few times," Cecilia says. "When I feel I need to remember someone, I 'rehearse' that person's features and name over and over again. If I don't rehearse, I do not remember the looks of the person at all." The two groups of people Cecilia feels most comfortable with are those she knows very well and complete strangers. When she's traveling, for instance, she feels comfort in knowing that there's little chance of running into people that she "should" recognize.

In 1992—when Cecilia was twenty-five—she discovered the medical term for face blindness, prosopagnosia, and anxiously set out to learn more. Unfortunately, the only cases referenced in the medical journals that she read involved people "who were so badly afflicted by face blindness and other conditions that they could barely function in society." This wasn't her experience. She did learn, however, that there was no cure for the condition—a fact that remains true today.

Discouraged, Cecilia shelved her research for years, ready to accept what she believed was her unique plight. Then in the spring of 2000, she found a book on the Internet called *Face Blind*, written by Bill Choisser, a San Francisco man who, among other things, was unable to recognize his mother when he passed within two feet of her in a neighborhood shopping district!

Finally, Cecilia had found someone who understood her condition. "It was such a relief that for weeks I couldn't talk about it without tears welling up," she says. "I immediately showed *Face Blind* to my husband and then two days later to his parents. Within hours I felt that they actually understood my problem—as much as you can understand without experiencing it yourself."

Today, Cecilia hosts a Web site to educate people about face blindness and to share her story. She's also part of an Internet mailing list called "The Face Blind Folks," where people discuss everything from how they discovered they were face blind to how and when to tell others about their condition. "Until a few years ago, I had been completely alone in my problem," says Cecilia. "Now when I am in contact with other prosopagnosics, it's as if a great weight is being lifted."

LANGUAGE OF EXPRESSIONS

SMILES. SMIRKS. STARES.

Faces communicate a rich language all their own. While crocodiles command only four facial expressions, humans boast an intricately woven set of facial muscles that allows us to make as many as 10,000 different expressions. Only about seven appear to be biologically based and universally recognized—anger, happiness, disgust, surprise, fear, sadness, and contempt—but many variations exist.

From birth, humans exhibit emotions. During the first three months of life,

Babies display a variety of facial expressions from birth.

babies scrunch their faces and cry in distress, squint and wrinkle their noses when they're disgusted, and raise their rosy cheeks in a smile when they're happy. By three to nine months, babies begin to show anger and fear—expressions that unfold naturally as they gain an initial understanding of the world around them. These basic emotions are innate. We know because even children who have been blind since birth and have never seen a face exhibit joy, sadness, fear, and anger just as other infants do. Such skills help babies build strong bonds and bring out the nurturing instinct in their caregivers during the fragile first months of life.

While babies express emotions, they also read them. Infants as young as ten weeks old respond to a range of emotions, from happiness to sadness to anger. This is how they begin the delicate dance of interacting with people.

* * * * * *

White Lies and Alibis

"THANKS FOR the purple polka-dotted sweater," you say to your grandmother with a smile. But what kind of smile are you expressing? If it's a sweater you've been hoping for, you've probably communicated a "true" smile of enjoyment—a smile that not only contracts the muscles that raise the cheeks and pulls up the corners of your lips, but also activates the outer part of the muscle circling your eyes. If you're not so crazy about the sweater or polka dots, you've probably put on a polite smile—a lips-only social smile that masks your true thoughts and keeps Grandma's feelings from being hurt.

People smile when they're happy and when they're not so happy, says Dr. Paul Ekman, a leading psychologist who has studied emotions and facial expressions for more than thirty years. But of the eighteen or so varieties of smiles that Dr. Ekman has identified, he says there is only one true smile that springs from genuine enjoyment. All other smiles are "non-enjoyment smiles" that we generally use to smooth social interactions.

Unlike the social-smoothing smile, the true smile cannot be imitated easily. It's involuntary, and in most cases, you've got to feel it on the inside to produce it, says Dr. Ekman. "Actors who convincingly look as if they are enjoying themselves are either among that small group who can contract the outer part of the muscle voluntarily (about 10 percent of us), or, more likely, they are retrieving a memory that generates the emotion, which then produces the true involuntary expression."

If actors and others can sometimes fake expressions, how can we tell when someone's lying to us? Half the time we can't, says Dr. Ekman, in his book *Emotions Revealed*. He found that most of us—including police officers and judges—have only a 50/50 chance

Actor Jim Carrey is a master of facial expressions.

of spotting a liar and that the only people who consistently detected liars were Secret Service Agents. What clues do they pick up in people's faces that the rest of us miss?

"Micro expressions," says Dr. Ekman. Micro expressions are fleeting facial expressions that last less than one-fifth of a second but that reveal emotions people are trying to conceal. They're involuntary "slips of the face," so people aren't even aware that they're making them. While we may smile and say to a friend, "I'm happy that you received a puppy for your birthday," our face may flash a brief, authentic signal of envy that says, "But I wish I had one, too."

One unexpected benefit that Dr. Ekman and other researchers have discovered about faking expressions is that if you "put on a happy face" when you're sad, it can lift your mood. Emotions not only affect our facial expressions, our facial expressions affect and adjust our emotions.

In one study, researchers found that when people made angry and sad facial expressions, their heart rate increased and their body temperature rose as if they were experiencing stress. Another showed that people who imitate the facial expressions of others are better able to empathize with them and feel what they're feeling. If you literally want to "feel someone else's pain," you can start by imitating their facial expressions.

SPECIAL SMILES

Facial expressions say much about who we are and how we're feeling, but some people are born with a condition called Moebius Syndrome, which prevents them from communicating to others with their face.

IMAGINE BEING born without the ability to smile. Without a way to express your happiness to your mom or dad, your brothers and sisters, or your friends. People with Moebius Syndrome come into the world without a smile.

Moebius Syndrome is a rare and little-known disorder that robs people of facial expressions because two important nerves—the sixth and seventh cranial nerves, which control eye muscle and face movements—are either inactive or not fully developed. This leaves the face paralyzed—unable to grin with delight or frown in sadness. In most cases, people with Moebius Syndrome cannot squint, blink, or move their eyes from side to side. Feeding can also be an issue for babies who have difficulty drinking from a bottle or breast. They require a special bottle called the Haberman feeder, which gently releases liquid into their mouth at the slightest touch of the tongue.

Vicki McCarrell's son, Sean, came into the world without a smile thirteen years ago, and she wasn't quite sure what to do.

Lauren Deveney before "smile surgery."

Lauren's kindergarten photo after the operations.

"You sneak peaks at your baby all day long, hoping to catch his first smile," Vicki says. "It never comes. Slowly, you realize it never will. You wonder how other children and adults will treat him. Then you search for other families affected by this rare occurrence."

That first year, Vicki found about thirty families affected by Moebius Syndrome, but no support group existed for the condition, so she and a friend, Lori Thomas—whose daughter Chelsea also has Moebius Syndrome—began publishing an informational newsletter in 1991. A few years later, they formed the Moebius Syndrome Foundation, which now involves about 1,000 families from around the world.

"Networking with others affected by Moebius Syndrome is vitally important," says Vicki. "Parents and children feel less alone." Through conferences and a Web site, they also learn about the latest treatments and techniques for dealing with the condition, including an operation affectionately called "smile surgery."

About 100 children and adults with Moebius have undergone the pioneering surgery recently developed by Dr. Ronald Zuker of the Hospital for Sick Children in Toronto, Canada—including Lauren Deveney.

While Lauren's parents, Dan and Sharon Deveney, knew Dr. Zuker couldn't revive their daughter's paralyzed nerve cells or cure Moebius Syndrome, they were hoping he could bring her a smile to help her emotionally connect with her classmates. "Our goal was for her to be smiling in kindergarten," Sharon says. So, in January 2000, when Lauren was five years old, the family traveled to Toronto for the first of two eight-hour surgeries.

"Dr. Zuker takes a part of the gracilis muscle from the inner thigh and implants it in the cheek," says Sharon. The muscle is carefully positioned so that when it contracts, it lifts the corner of the mouth and upper lip. Lauren learned to smile by biting down on the back of her teeth, says her mother. (Recently, doctors discovered that smile surgery patients do not need to bite down on the back of their teeth to form a smile. The nerves activate on their own after the operation.)

When the surgery on the left side of Lauren's face proved successful, Dr. Zuker operated on the right side in June 2000. By September, Lauren carried a smile with her to school—one she's been flashing proudly ever since.

MARKS OF BEAUTY

"If truth is beauty, how come no one has their hair done in a library?"
—*Comedian Lily Tomlin*

BEAUTIFUL FACES. People everywhere seem to want them. Cosmetic companies earn billions of dollars each year selling everything from lip gloss to pimple cream. Magazines feature attractive models and offer beauty tips on shaping eyebrows and accentuating cheekbones. Stylists design hair to frame the shape of the face, and color specialists match clothing to complement skin tones. To keep away wrinkles, some people exercise their face muscles or inject chemicals to stop folds from forming. Still others reshape their eyes, nose, and/or chin with plastic surgery.

Why do looks matter so much?

Biologically speaking, beauty is part of nature's plan for us to reproduce and survive as a species. Smooth skin, shiny hair, and healthy teeth turn heads. So do facial features that are in proportion to each other, as well as those that are symmetrical (the same on both sides of the face). Having such traits indicates to potential mates that we're healthy and will produce strong children. A woman's young-looking face also implies fertility.

Beauty is as important to us as food and water, suggests Dr. Nancy Etcoff in her book, *Survival of the Prettiest: The Science of Beauty*. One sign that a person is depressed is a lack of response to beautiful things.

However, beauty is not only biological. It's also an idea based in the eye of the beholder. Many factors influence it, including our families, culture, customs, economic status, and the media. As history shows, we've been fascinated by facial beauty for centuries.

Beauty through the Ages

THE ANCIENT Egyptians, who lived from about 3300 to 30 B.C., meticulously painted their faces, creating almond-shaped eyes with a dark pigment called kohl, reddening their cheeks and lips with rouge, and slipping on stylish black wigs over their shaved heads. Roman men and women circa 400 A.D. dyed their hair blond and viewed the unibrow—eyebrows that meet over the nose—as a sign of beauty.

In the middle ages, upper-class European women bled themselves to look pale, so that others saw they were "rich enough not to work outdoors." Meanwhile, Asian women painted their faces white and blackened their teeth. In Japan, tooth blackening, known as *ohagura*, was practiced to make a woman more appealing, while chemicals in

In Japan, Geisha girls paint their faces white and their lips red to enhance their beauty.

the blackening solution helped prevent tooth decay. The Vietnamese also blackened their teeth, but for different reasons. They believed that only wild animals and demons had long, white teeth, and they didn't want to be mistaken for evil spirits.

In Elizabethan England, red hair was the rage, along with thinly plucked eyebrows and "spacious" foreheads—a look many achieved by shaving back the hair at the top of their heads. During the fifteenth and sixteenth centuries, face makeup contained lead that sometimes paralyzed women's muscles or contributed to their deaths. By the seventeenth century, chubby faces—complete with double chins—were in. Two centuries later, during the Victorian era, the natural look of little to no makeup ruled, as people believed brightly painted faces were sinful.

It wasn't until the 1920s that makeup became popular among the masses, especially in the United States, when women gained the right to vote. Soon, tanned faces replaced pale ones as the standard of beauty, and Hollywood stars began dictating facial fashions. Today, many women—and an increasing number of men—imitate the hairstyles and makeup of movie stars, pop singers, and celebrities from all walks of life.

Many children enjoy having their faces painted at community events. This "lion" looks ready to roar!

Face Painting and Tattoos

LOOKING GOOD isn't the only reason we paint our faces. Often, it's part of a ritual, a means of identification, or a way to convey social messages. We paint children's faces at fairs and as part of Halloween costumes. During World Cup games, many soccer fans paint their country's flag on their faces. Protesters use the face as a canvas to communicate their strong feelings.

Historically, Native Americans painted their faces for camouflage when hunting, before battles to look fierce, and as part of special ceremonies such as powwows. The importance of the face also is reflected in Native American totem poles, which display the wood-carved features of people and animals to communicate tribal stories.

A more permanent type of face decorating is tattooing. Most people who wear tattoos have them on their bodies, but some, such as the Maori men of New Zealand, wore specially designed tattoos in an art form called *Moko* on their faces. The following description is from the University of Pennsylvania Museum of Archaeology and Anthropology:

The Maori tribesmen of New Zealand used **Moko** to distinguish between different social classes.

The pattern was literally carved into the skin with a chisel, much the way designs are carved into wood. Ink would be placed in the cuts to create the tattoo. The process, which was extremely painful, was typically done in stages, starting in early adulthood. Maori facial tattoos were indications of power and prestige, designed to impress and intimidate, especially in battle. Since no two patterns were alike, men's facial tattoos were also markers of individual identity.

Closely related to Maori tattooing is the art of scarification—puncturing the skin in patterns to create raised scars. Many African men and women associate scarification with beauty and bravery. A young woman who bears facial scars communicates to others in her group that she is courageous and emotionally ready to endure the pain of childbirth.

· · · · · ·

Piercing

ANOTHER POPULAR form of face decorating is piercing. While some people pierce their noses, tongues, and eyebrows, the most common form is ear-piercing, which has been practiced throughout history. In fact, figurines of faces from 4,000 years ago display holes for multiple ear piercings.

The Tlingit people of southeast Alaska used ear piercings as a way to display a person's rank in society. To raise a child's status in the community, relatives held community feasts called potlatches and paid someone from their group to pierce the child's ears. The more potlatches held and the more holes added to the child's ears, the more noble he became.

Stretching the earlobes to accommodate ear spools and plugs also dates back centuries, as do lip and nose piercing. Nose rings are worn on either side of the nose or through the middle and were also viewed by the Tlingit people as a mark of prestige. Today they remain especially popular in countries such as India and Pakistan.

SAVING FACES

"LEND ME your eyes and ears," the teacher called to her class.

"Which one do you want?" replied Michael Munds, unclipping a prosthetic ear from the side of his head. Not exactly what his teacher had in mind, but the fourteen-year-old from Denver, Colorado, likes to maintain a sense of humor about his situation.

Michael was born with Treacher Collins Syndrome, a genetic condition that affects the head and face. People with Treacher Collins Syndrome generally display characteristics such as downward-slanting eyes, a small lower jaw, underdeveloped cheekbones, and malformed or missing ears. Most who are affected, like Michael, possess normal intelligence. However, their appearance can sometimes lead people to believe otherwise.

During Michael's elementary school years, surgeons reconstructed his cheekbones and his chin from parts of his ribs. But they could not replace his missing ears. That job eventually would fall to Barbara Spohn-Lillo. Spohn-Lillo is an anaplastologist who uses her knowledge of art, anatomy, and science to create custom prostheses (artificial parts) for people with facial disfigurements.

"My work begins when the doctors can no longer help," says Spohn-Lillo, who is also an ocularist—a person who makes artificial eyes. "Many of my patients have pretty severe facial deformities, so my job is to try to help them create an illusion"—such as the look of a real eye or nose or ear, so that patients can feel good about themselves and easily blend in during social situations. "Ultimately, the goal is for people to listen to what my clients say and not be distracted by how they look."

Some of Spohn-Lillo's clients have lost facial features to cancer, severe burns, diseases, or accidents. Others, like Michael, were born without them. With the help of a bone-anchored hearing aid that snaps in the back of his head, Michael can hear pretty well. That's because the inner workings of his ears remain intact, despite the absence of their outer coverings. After several attempts to create ears from his own tissue, doctors recommended that Michael wear prosthetic ears. Even then it took a few tries to get it right. "His first set needed a lot of glue to stay on," explains his mother, Gayle Munds, "and the second set looked fake and popped off every time he turned his head."

When Michael visited Spohn-Lillo at Prosthetic Illusions, she "listened to what he had to say" about how his new ears fit. Now Michael has ears that "feel natural and look like everyone else's."

* * * * * *

Master of Illusion

SPOHN-LILLO began honing her unique craft at age sixteen, when she apprenticed with her father, the director of a special joint anaplastology and ocular program offered by Stanford University Medical Center and the state of California. "I grew up with [fake] body parts all over the house," she says, "and I found I had a knack for this work." Today she carries on the legacy of her father, helping people rebuild their faces and their lives.

The process begins when Spohn-Lillo meets with clients in her lab to learn more about them and their expectations. "Some of the stories can be very sad," she says. One man's nose was burned in a car accident; another lost his to cancer. When making a facial feature such as a nose or an ear, Spohn-Lillo considers her client's preferences for shape as well as the proportions of his or her face. If they are available, she also uses old photos of the person as a reference point and collects information from family members.

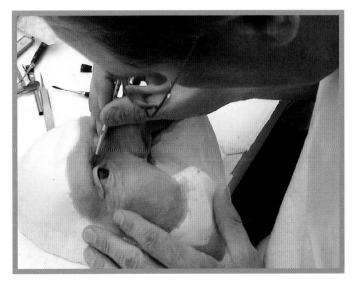

A prosthetic face is molded around the eyes.

Next she creates a plaster cast of the person's face and uses the model to form the missing feature in wax. She fits the wax model on her client and adjusts its shape until she's ready to make a mold of it in dental stone. When the mold is complete, she pours silicone material in it to create the artificial part, which she later tailors to the client. During this time, she paints the prosthesis to match the person's skin tone and adds realistic details to it, such as freckles.

When creating artificial eyes, she weaves tiny strands of red silk thread on the acrylic replica and delicately paints the iris with varying shades of blues, browns, or greens. Where needed, she also fashions eyebrows and eyelashes from the hair or feathers of moose, elk, rabbit, and roosters, which she buys at a fly-fishing store. If all goes well, the work takes about two to three weeks to complete.

"It's very satisfying because I get to see the end result," says Spohn-Lillo. "And I can see that people feel better about themselves in their physical demeanor." To help boost her clients' confidence in a crowd, Spohn-Lillo suggests that they wear glasses to make their new eyes and noses look more natural, and slip on earrings to disguise their prosthetic ears. "It's part of creating the whole look," she says, so that they feel comfortable interacting with others and people feel comfortable talking with them.

The "Butterfly baby" and her parents after several operations to rebuild the toddler's face from disfigurements.

Best Face Forward

WHILE FACIAL differences may be scary and temporarily turn heads in most cultures, they can ruin lives in others. That's one reason Spohn-Lillo volunteers with a nonprofit group called Face the Challenge, and visits Vietnam each year with a team of doctors, nurses, and other specialists who devote their skills to repairing children's severe facial deformities. "It's really important that we work with these children and fix their faces," she says. "It not only improves their health, but helps keep them from being ostracized by people in their communities who believe they are cursed by an evil spirit. Without the surgery [and prostheses], many of these children would become beggars and live on the streets."

To prevent their children from being shunned, parents save money all year and travel many miles to meet the Face the Challenge team when it arrives at Ho Chi Minh City. "It's a major event for these people," says Spohn-Lillo. "About one hundred fifty or so stand in line for surgeries, and we're able to complete about half. Some need multiple surgeries and come back year after year for follow-ups."

One little girl close to Spohn-Lillo's heart is nicknamed the "butterfly baby," a nickname given to her by a nurse because when the flaps of her face were folded out during surgery, they looked like the wings of a butterfly. "When we first met her a couple of years ago, she barely looked human and her parents hid her from others. The next year [after her first surgery] she had pigtails and was playing with other kids. I can't wait to see what she looks like now when we go back there."

More Face Facts to Explore

PUBLICATIONS

Bug Faces, by Darlyne A. Murawski. New York: National Geographic, 2000.

Decorate Yourself: Cool Designs for Temporary Tattoos, Face Painting, Henna & More, by Tom Andrich. New York: Sterling/Tamos, 2003.

EyeOpeners!, by Monika Dossenbach and Hans D. Dossenback. San Diego: Blackbirch Marketing, 1998.

The Face, by Daniel McNeill. New York: Little, Brown and Company, 1998.

The Human Face, by Brian Bates with John Cleese. London: Dorling Kindersley Publishing, Inc., 2001.

The Looks Book: A Whole New Approach to Beauty, Body Image, and Style, by Rebecca Odes, Esther Drill, and Heather McDonald. New York: Penguin Books, 2002.

WEB SITES

American Museum of Natural History—Body Art: Marks of Identity Online Exhibit: www.amnh.org/exhibitions/bodyart/exhibition_highlights.html

Cecilia Burman's Prosopagnosia (Face-Blindness) Site: www.prosopagnosia.com

Face the Challenge: Organization that surgically corrects facial deformities of the youngest and poorest in the world. www.facethechallenge.org

The Moebius Syndrome Foundation: www.ciaccess.com/moebius/main.htm

National Center for Missing & Exploited Children: www.missingkids.com

University of Pennsylvania—Bodies of Culture Online Exhibit: www.museum.upenn.edu/new/exhibits/online_exhibits/body_modification/bodmodintro.shtml

Face Glossary

Anaplastologist: a person who specializes in making artificial face and body parts.

Biometrics: technologies that identify people based on features such as the face, eyes, and fingerprints.

DNA (deoxyribonucleic acid): the chemical blueprint that makes us who we are.

FaceIt: a facial recognition technology that identifies people by measuring facial landmarks.

Facial prosthesis: an artificial device used to replace a missing or malformed facial feature.

Forensic imaging specialist: a person who uses art, science, photos, and a computer to progressively age someone who has been missing for several years or more.

Genes: stretches of DNA stored in each of our cells that carry traits, such as eye color, from parents to children.

Homo sapiens: the modern species of humans.

IBIS (identification-based information system): a hand-held tool used to identify people based on their facial features.

Innate: describes a characteristic present from birth.

Kohl: a dark cosmetic pigment used by the ancient Egyptians to line their eyes.

Melanin: dark pigments found in our skin, hair, and eyes.

Micro expressions: term developed by psychologist Paul Ekman to describe fleeting facial expressions lasting less than one-fifth of a second, which reveal emotions that people are trying to conceal.

Moebius Syndrome: a rare disorder that results in paralyzed facial muscles because two important nerves—the sixth and seventh cranial nerves, which control eye muscle and face movements—are either inactive or not fully developed.

Moko: an art form used to create special tattoos by the Maori peoples of New Zealand.

Nonenjoyment smiles: smiles we generally use in social situations, such as the polite smile and the grin-and-bear-it smile. These smiles do not activate the outer part of the muscle circling the eye.

Ocular prosthesis: artificial eye used to simulate a natural-looking eye.

Ocularist: a person who makes artificial eyes.

Ohagura: the Japanese practice of tooth-blackening.

Prosopagnosia: face blindness, a condition characterized by an inability to recognize faces—sometimes even your own. It can be present at birth or caused later in life by a stroke or accident involving the head.

Prosthesis: an artificial face or body part made to replace one that is missing, disfigured, or malformed.

Scarification: the process of puncturing the skin to create raised scars. In some cultures, it signifies a rite of passage into adulthood and the ability to endure pain.

Smile surgery: a pioneering operation developed by Dr. Ronald Zuker of the Hospital for Sick Children in Toronto, Canada, that positions the facial muscles so that they can form a smile.

Symmetrical features: features that are proportionally even on both sides of the face.

Tattoos: pictures or designs on the skin that are made by pricking and staining it with permanent color.

Tilaka: a bright red mark on the forehead worn by people of the Hindu religion.

Treacher Collins Syndrome: a genetic condition affecting the head and face and characterized by underdeveloped cheekbones and malformed or missing ears.

True smile: a smile of enjoyment that activates the outer part of the muscle circling the eyes.

Source Notes

ABOUT FACE

ABOUT FACE; TOUR DE FACE: Daniel McNeill, *The Face* (New York: Little, Brown and Co., 1998), pp. 12–76; Brian Bates with John Cleese, *The Human Face* (London: Dorling Kindersley Publishing, Inc., 2001), pp. 14–36; Dr. Steven Denenberg's Web site at www.facialsurgery.com.

FACIAL IDENTITY

FIRST IMPRESSIONS: Bates, pp. 44–49; Interview with Leslie Zebrowitz, author of *Reading Faces: Window to the Soul?*; Amanda Onion, "You're So Striking (Just Like Me)," abcNEWS.com, June 28, 2002.

OVERGENERALIZING TRAITS: Interview with Leslie Zebrowitz; Leslie A. Zebrowitz, *Reading Faces: Window to the Soul?* (Boulder, Col.: Westview Press, 1997), pp. 14–39, 56, 64–82, 84.

MISSING FACES: Interview with Steve Loftin and S. Orname Thompson of the National Center for Missing & Exploited Children (www.missingkids.com).

FACIAL RECOGNITION: Vicki Bruce and Andy Young, *In the Eye of the Beholder: The Science of Face Perception* (Oxford: Oxford University Press, 1998), pp. 66–88.

FACEPRINTS: Interviews with Meir Kahtan of Identix, Inc. (www.identix.com) and Beverly Griffin of Griffin Investigations; Emelie Rutherford, "Facial Recognition has People Pegged," CNN.com, July 17, 2001.

UNFAMILIAR FACES

Interview with Cecilia Burman and review of her Web site at www.prosopagnosia.com.

Interview with Dr. Bradley Duchaine of the Vision Sciences Laboratory at Harvard University.

Bill Choisser, *Face Blind*, Internet book at www.choisser.com/faceblind.

LANGUAGE OF EXPRESSIONS

Bates, pp. 80, 88; Paul Ekman, *Emotions Revealed: Recognizing Faces and Feelings to Improve Communication and Emotional Life* (New York: Times Books, Henry Holt and Company, 2003), pp. 1–16, 204–212; Malcolm Gladwell, "The Naked Face: Can You Read People's Thoughts Just by Looking at Them?" *The New Yorker*, Aug. 5, 2002; David G. Myers, *Psychology: 6th Edition* (New York: Worth Publishers), pp. 475–476.

SPECIAL SMILES

Interviews with Vicki McCarrell of the Moebius Syndrome Foundation (www.moebiussyndrome.com) and Sharon Deveney (www.geocities.com/heartland/hills/5897), and a review of their Web sites.

MARKS OF BEAUTY

BEAUTY, BALANCE, AND BIOLOGY: Nancy Etcoff, *Survival of the Prettiest: The Science of Beauty* (New York: Doubleday, 1999), p. 8.

BEAUTY THROUGH THE AGES: Barbara Cohen, "Healthy Black Smiles," www.thingsasian.com, Jan. 1, 2000; Richard Corson, *Fashions in Makeup* (London: Peter Owen Limited, 1972), pp. 8–23; 51–63, 93–111, 315–321; Kathy Peiss, *Hope in a Jar: The Making of America's Beauty Culture* (New York: Henry Holt and Company, 1998), pp. 134–166.

FACE PAINTING AND TATTOOS; PIERCING: University of Pennsylvania Museum of Archaeology and Anthropology "Bodies of Culture" exhibit at: www.museum.upenn.edu/new/exhibits/online_exhibits/body_modification/bodmodintro.shtml.

SAVING FACES

Interviews with Barbara Spohn-Lillo at Prosthetic Illusions (www.prostheticillusions.com), Gayle and Michael Munds, and David Trainer (www.factor2.com). Review of Face the Challenge Web site at www.facethechallenge.org.

Index

Face to face

Cat got your to[ngue]

Face the music

Fight tooth

In your face

Right under your nose

Beauty is only skin d[eep]

Play by ear

Lead with your chin

Two-faced

Ga[me]

Eyes in the back of h[ead]

Game face

In the blink of an eye

The hairy

Eye for an eye

Baby face

Thun[der]

I'[m]

Stone-faced

Tongue-

I'm all ears

Got my

Sight for sore eyes

Plain as the

Tripped on his tong[ue]

My ears are burning

Apple of my eye

Ju[st]

Dancing cheek to cheek

Pull the wool over your eyes

Face the facts

In your face

face

Sla[p]

Got my eye on you

Win by a nose

Poker face

On the tip

The nose knows

Tripped on

On the tip of his tongue

I'm

Living hand to mouth

Keep your

Apple of my eye

By the skin of your teeth